POSTPARTUM
IS A MOTHER

CHYNA EDGHILL

Welcome to the fire and the softness.
You belong here.
This is your space to fall apart and rise again. To feel it all.
To be held in the mess and the magic.
This is your becoming.

About The Author

Chyna Edghill is a creator, writer, and businesswoman rooted in resilience, motherhood, and grace. A mama of two, a proud fire wife, and the heart behind Postpartum is a Mother, she brings her lived experience, raw truth, and deep compassion to the page.

She's not here to sugarcoat. She's here to hold space — for the breakdowns, the rebuilding, and the rising. Her writing is both a soft place to land and a powerful push forward. With a calm voice and fire soul, Chyna invites every reader into a space that says, "You're not broken. You're becoming."

When she's not writing, you'll find her in her "denim and latte era," running her small businesses, chasing after her babies, or sitting by the fire with her family. She lives in the balance of soft and strong — where the feminine divine meets everyday life.

This is her offering. Her truth. Her story — and maybe yours too.

Dedication

For HER.

The one becoming.

The one breaking and rebuilding.

The one whispering prayers between feedings, holding it all together with one shaky hand and a whole lot of heart.

This is for the mama who's in it.

Who's felt the shift.

Who's rising in quiet ways no one sees.

You are not just surviving —

You are transforming.

To HER — this is your book.

This is your homecoming.

Acknowledgment

To God — thank you for holding me when I couldn't hold myself. You carried me through the nights that broke me and the mornings that made me.

To my husband, Jason — my anchor, my safe place, my Team Me. You never judged me. You never walked away. Your love didn't flinch, and because of that, I didn't fall apart. Thank you for seeing me when I couldn't see myself.

To my babies, Mason and Riley — you are my why. Every word in this book was written from the depths of love I found in mothering you. I gave up a lot for you, but not swearing — and not this truth. You made me a mother. You made me real.

To my Memere, Carole David — your strength lives in me. You taught me how to keep going. How to believe. How to have faith in the dark.

To my sisters, my friends, my soul circle — you know who you are. The ones who listened, prayed, dragged me out of bed, sent voice notes, made me laugh, and reminded me I wasn't crazy — just postpartum. I love you.

To the mamas who messaged me, cried with me, shared their stories — this is for you. This is yours. Thank you for trusting me to write it.

And to every mother reading this — I see you. I love you. I'm standing beside you in spirit. This book was never just about me. It was always about us.

Sincerely,
Chyna Edghill

Contents

Chapter 1

Postpartum Hits Different

Nobody warned me about the ambush.
Not just in my body — but in my mind, my soul, my spirit.

Postpartum didn't tap politely.
It hit.
Like a f**king freight train.

You think you'll be tired.
You think you'll cry.
You know your body will be sore, and that sleep will be a
stranger.
But nothing — nothing — prepares you for the emotional
ricochet that follows birth.

This is the chapter no one writes.
The one nobody dares to post about.
Because it's not pretty.
It's not filtered.
And it sure as hell doesn't come with a bow.

Postpartum is not just about a baby being born.
It's about a woman breaking apart and rebuilding from the
inside out.
It's about the version of you that existed before —
and how she doesn't quite fit anymore.

You can look at your baby with a love so deep it hurts,
and still feel like you're drowning.

You can be grateful, and resentful.
Joyful, and hollow.
Tender, and enraged — all in the same breath.
That's not failure.
That's postpartum.

You will feel love.
But you may also feel rage.
The kind that bubbles from nowhere, sharp and hot.
The kind that makes you question your goodness —
even though you're giving everything you have.

You will feel grief.
Grief for your old life.
Your old body.
Your old self —
the one who didn't hesitate before she left the house.
The one who could hear herself think.

You will miss her.
And you will also outgrow her.

Because this isn't a soft chapter.
This is the reckoning.
The cracking open.
The sacred unraveling.

You won't just become a mother.
You'll meet every shadow you've ever avoided.
Your triggers.
Your wounds.
Your deepest fears.
All of it.
And still — you'll show up.
Because that's what we do.

But let me be the one to say it:
You're not ungrateful.
You're not dramatic.
You're not crazy.
You're not failing.

You're a woman —
becoming.

This book?
It's Rated R —
For Rebuilding. Rebirth. Realness.

Because what you're living through isn't just a season.
It's a storm.
And still, you rise.

I wish someone had told me…
That postpartum would test every part of me.
That my body wouldn't feel like mine.
That I'd cry in the dark and still wake up to do it all again.

I wish someone had told me that this might be the loneliest I'd ever feel.
Even in a house full of love.
Even with a baby in my arms.
Even with a partner beside me.

Because postpartum doesn't care how strong you are.
It strips you down anyway.
And then?
It hands you pieces of yourself you didn't know were missing.

This is the part no one wants to talk about.
The part where the "fourth trimester" feels more like a free fall.
Where your hormones hijack your peace.
Where your nervous system is lit up like the Rockefeller tree.
Where a loud toy, a wrong look, or a skipped nap can send you spiraling.

This is the part where brushing your teeth feels like a win.
Where folding laundry makes you cry.
Where you put your baby down and immediately miss them
— but don't want to hold them either.
Where your insides ache for rest, for space, for you —
but you can't quite figure out where she went.

This is the chapter that holds you tight and says:
You're not alone in this madness.
You're not wrong for feeling this way.
And you are still worthy of love, even when you don't recognize yourself.

Your softness is sacred.
Your rage is holy.
Your exhaustion is valid.
And your strength?
Unmatched.

Say it with me:
"Postpartum didn't ruin me — it revealed me."

Question for You:
• What has surprised you the most about postpartum?
• What emotion has been the loudest?
• What truth have you been too scared to say out loud?

Pause & Process Page:
Say the quiet part.
The raw part.
The "I thought I was the only one" part.
Write it. Scream it. Cry it. Whisper it.
This is where healing begins.

Flip the Page…

If postpartum was the emotional ambush,
then what came next —
the bleeding, breaking, unraveling —
would demand more than I thought I had left.

But even in the rubble,
a new woman began to rise.

Let's keep going.

This isn't just about what happens emotionally after you
become a mother.

It's what happens physically —
when your body, your cycles, your hormones, your organs,
and your intuition all start screaming at the same time...

And nobody listens.

Because postpartum doesn't care about your plans.
It doesn't stick to timelines.
It doesn't read the books or follow the rules.

It just comes for you.

And once the emotional ambush hits...
the physical battle begins.

Because what came next for me wasn't just exhaustion or
hormones.
It was bleeding.
It was burnout.
It was my body begging me to listen.

Her story's just getting started.

Chapter 2

Rated R — Real & Raw

There are parts of postpartum no one prepares you for.
Not just the tears or the rage.
Not just the identity shift or the mental spiral.
But the physical unraveling —
the ways your body keeps the score… and the scar.

For me, it started long before motherhood.
Long before anyone cared to ask why I was hurting.
Long before doctors took my pain seriously.

I've been bleeding most of my life — in more ways than one.
And for too long, no one cared enough to figure out why.

I was 13 when it started.
Heavy. Relentless. Dismissed.
The solution? Birth control. Over and over again.
Pill after pill. Shot after shot.
Not healing — just silencing.

Eventually, I tried hormone replacement therapy and finally
started to feel a little more human again.

But that battle was far from over.

Because somehow, after all that, my body still gave me two
babies — two absolute miracles.

Two reminders that maybe my body wasn't broken after all.

And then, right after baby number two, it betrayed me again.

The bleeding returned.

This time, it wasn't teenage confusion — it was a full-grown woman, a mother,
whose body had been pushed past the edge.
And still, no one listened. No one looked deeper.
I was sent home with the same answers I'd always been given:

"It's normal."
"Your hormones are still shifting."
"Try another pill."
"You look great!"

(Yeah. I "looked great" because I was bleeding out and withering away while training like hell just to feel like I had control of something.)

But my physical strength? It was the tip of the iceberg.

Because underneath all of that muscle was a woman crumbling — mentally, emotionally, spiritually.

And still, I kept going. Because I had to.

Because even when the system dismissed me, I refused to dismiss myself.

This chapter?
It's Rated R for Real and Raw.
Because what I went through wasn't gentle.
It was war. It was lonely. It was brutal.

But it was also the beginning of my rising.

Eventually, I found a surgeon. A real one.
A woman at a top-tier hospital who finally looked me in the
eyes and said: "You've been through enough."

And with her guidance, we chose the path forward — a
hysterectomy.

At 37, I let it all go. The bleeding. The confusion. The fight
to be heard.

And for the first time in decades, I felt free.

It wasn't a loss — it was a relief of epic proportions.

This body of mine had taken a beating.
It had been silenced, overlooked, overmedicated, and still —
she showed up.

Still, she gave life.
Still, she held me together.
Still, she whispered, "Keep going."

And I did.

Not because I always believed I could.

But because I had the faith of a mustard seed — and
sometimes, that's more than enough.

I wasn't just fighting for me. I was fighting for the mother I
knew I could be.
The woman my babies deserved.
The wife my husband never stopped believing in.
The me who would not go quietly.

This wasn't a phase. It wasn't "just hormones."
This was my body screaming. And I finally listened.

If you're there now — confused, dismissed, afraid to push
back — I need you to know this:

Your body is not a burden.
Your pain is not imaginary.
And your voice is not too loud.

It's not in your head.

It's in your bones.
In your blood.
And in your birthright to be well.

Let them call you difficult.
Let them say it's "just part of motherhood."

And then — let them watch you rise.

One to live by:
"They told me I was fine. But my body knew better.
She led me to the truth — and I followed her all the way
home."
— A mother who refused to be silenced

Question for You:
• When did you first feel like something was off?
• Have you ever been dismissed or doubted?
• What would you say to a woman going through that now?

Pause & Process Page:
Real talk only.
Tell your truth. No filters. No shame.

Chapter 3

Heart Wide Open — My Heart Is Now Outside My Body

There's no manual for loving three soulmates at once.

There's no guidebook for how to give your whole heart to a husband, a son, and a daughter — while scraping together something soft and salvageable to give yourself too.

When my daughter was born, my heart didn't just expand.

It cracked open.
It burst.
It rearranged itself in ways I never saw coming.

I didn't just have one baby to love anymore.

I had two.

Mason was born in July 2020, and for a while, I thought I understood what it meant to love a child so deeply it restructured your entire being. But when Riley arrived in July 2022, my heart cracked open again—wider, deeper, wilder. I wasn't just mothering one little soul anymore. I was holding two. And learning to hold myself, too.

I had a husband who had been my home base and my safe landing long before babies came into the picture.

And somewhere inside the fog of sleep deprivation, hormone crashes, rage bursts, bleeding, and survival-mode mothering…

I was still supposed to love me too.

But how?

There's no equation for love in postpartum.
It's not 33% for him, 33% for my son, 33% for my daughter.
It's never equal, and it's rarely gentle.

Some days, someone got the best of me.
Some days, someone else got the rest of me.
And some days, I didn't even recognize myself in the mirror
— hollow-eyed, overstretched, and drowning in guilt.

Because how do you love everyone the way they deserve…
when you're barely surviving yourself?

Neuroscience Note: The Maternal Brain's Transformation

"During the postpartum period, the brain undergoes significant neuroplastic changes, particularly in regions such as the amygdala and prefrontal cortex. These changes enhance emotional regulation and responsiveness, effectively rewiring the brain to prioritize caregiving behaviors and maternal sensitivity."
— Chechko et al., Nature Translational Psychiatry, 2023

It's not failure.
It's biology.
You're not broken — you're becoming something new.

We don't talk about this enough.

We're not encouraged to speak out loud about the emotional calculus that comes with loving your husband, your children, and yourself — all at once, all the time.

Especially when love doesn't show up neat and tidy.
Especially when guilt tries to drown it.
Especially when the world expects you to "just know how."

I didn't grow up in a home where love was loud.
Affection wasn't the currency we passed around.
I became emotionally self-sufficient.
I learned to thrive with very little softness.

But then came my husband.

His love was fluent in presence, patience, and protection.
He taught me that affection doesn't have to be earned.
That softness can be strong.
That I didn't have to survive everything alone.

He taught me how to let love in — not just offer it.

Loving my husband — the man who saw all the versions of me and stayed.

Loving my son — the one who made me a mother.
Loving my daughter — the one who cracked me wide open
again.

She's part me, part him. Fierce and tender, wild and soft.

And holding her?
It brought up things I didn't know I still carried.

Fears.
Old wounds.
Silent memories I thought I'd buried.

And in that same breath — she made me want to become
someone even safer, even softer, even stronger… for her.

Because having a daughter will split you open in ways no one
explains.
It makes you hyperaware of every harm you ever experienced
— and determined to shield her from every single one.

There's a wild, wordless devotion that kicks in.
A vow you whisper every time you brush her hair or watch
her sleep:

"It stops with me.
The silence.
The shame.
The hardness.
It ends here."

"When you never learned how to be loved out loud, raising a daughter becomes a revolutionary act. You teach her what you never got to receive — and in doing so, you heal yourself too."
— Tanya Markul

Loving myself?
That's still a work in progress.
But I've got the faith of a mustard seed — and some days, that's all it takes.

"You try to do everything at 100%, but the truth is, you have to make peace with the ebb and flow. Some days you give more here, some days more there, and that's okay."
— Michelle Obama

I didn't balance it perfectly.
I never will.

But my heart?
It lives outside my body now.
Stretching across every inch of the people I love most — and still, somehow, coming back to me too.

Question for You:
Where have you been hardest on yourself about loving your family?
What moments have taught you that love doesn't have to look perfect?

Pause & Process Page:
Write the messy parts.
Write the tender parts.
Write the parts you thought no one would understand.

Chapter 4

Peace In Pieces — My Survival Stack

This wasn't a picture-perfect recovery plan.

There were no vision boards, no timelines, no "get better by this date" checklist.

What I had were moments.
Tiny, gritty, sacred ones.
Pieces that grounded me when I was falling apart.

It wasn't polished.
It wasn't linear.

But it was real.

And it helped me build peace—one piece at a time.

Faith Over Fixes

Some days, all I had was instinct.
Other days, it was faith the size of a mustard seed.
I didn't always believe things would get better.
But I kept showing up like they might.

That was enough.

"Faith it till you make it."
(And some days, that was the whole damn plan.)

1. Somatic Movement: The Body Holds the Story

I didn't discover somatic movement on my own.

I found The Workout Witch — Liz on Instagram — and
something in me lit up.
Her work was a lifeline. She made somatics make sense. She
explained what the body holds and how to safely move it out.
Her videos, her reminders, her energy — they were essential
to my healing.

Thanks to her, I learned to move with purpose:
Gentle bouncing
Arm shaking
Side-to-side swaying
Reaching up and out to release what I couldn't name

Sometimes I'd picture the rage, the fear, the grief — all of it
— draining through my feet.
Back into the earth. Out of my body.

It wasn't a workout.
It was a reset. A return. A release.

And every single time, it reminded me:

I am not stuck. I am still moving. I am still healing.

2. Hygiene Rituals: Tethering Myself to the Day

Every day, I ended (or started) with a shower.

It didn't need to be long or luxurious — just five intentional minutes to wash off whatever the day had thrown at me. Tantrums. Overstimulation. Resentment. Guilt. Exhaustion. Big feelings.

It was how I released it.
It was how I reset.
It was how I carried on.

I always finished with cooler water, even if just for 30 seconds.
It helped bring down inflammation.
Calmed my nervous system.
Cleared the static in my body and mind.

That simple rinse wasn't just hygiene.
It was relief.
A quiet moment to shift into a better place.

3. Dressing to Calm the Chaos

Getting dressed stopped being about how I looked.
It became about how I felt.

A soft cotton tee over scratchy fabric.
The jeans that fit just right.
My favorite pajamas at night.
Lip gloss for no one but me.
A latte in hand like a warm reminder: this day is still mine.

Fashion psychology is real.
The clothing we wear either soothes or overstimulates.
And during postpartum, overstimulation is already on overdrive.

So when I dressed for softness and peace, I was choosing calm.
I was choosing me.

Even pajamas became an act of protection.
A reminder to my nervous system:
You can settle now.

4. Breathing to Expand and Release

I'm not here to preach breath work.

But I will say this:
Breath can move energy.

On days when my chest felt tight or my thoughts felt fast, I'd breathe with intention —
filling my lungs, expanding into my ribcage, giving my body a little shot of clarity.

That deep breath sometimes came with a hit of dopamine.
A quiet boost.
A release of pressure I didn't know I was holding.

Inhale.
Exhale.

Let go.

Not to fix everything — but to create space inside myself.

5. Prayer, Energy & Something Bigger Than Me

Some days, I didn't have words.
Just a feeling. A pleading. A silent request.

I wasn't sure who I was talking to — but I knew something bigger was listening.

The universe.
Divine energy.
Faith.
Something beyond the chaos.

I didn't need a church.
I didn't need a perfect prayer.

I just needed presence.
Honesty.
Hope.

And that presence never let me go.

Faith didn't erase the pain.
But it helped me move through it.

6. Love That Let Me Be Me

My husband didn't need me to smile.

He didn't need me to "bounce back."
He didn't expect perfection.

He stood beside the mess.
Held the tension.
Loved me in the in-between.

And so did my people — the friends I could text with no
filter.
The ones who didn't need small talk or updates.
Just truth.

Sometimes, healing doesn't come from what you do.
It comes from who stays when you can't give anything back.

This chapter isn't about transformation.
It's about survival.

The kind that doesn't always look pretty.
The kind that's made of tiny, stubborn, sacred pieces —
stacked one after another.

Breath by breath.
Choice by choice.
Peace by piece.

And one day, without even realizing it…

You're not holding yourself together anymore.

You're building something new.

"She didn't find peace all at once. She found it piece by piece
— and that was enough."
— A mama rebuilding herself for real

Question for You:
What small acts of survival are keeping you grounded right
now?
What does peace look like in your life today — even if it's
messy?
How can you honour your pieces without needing them to
look perfect?

Pause & Process Page:
Stack your survival.
Write the small wins.
Name the tiny pieces.
Claim your ground.

Postpartum Nervous System

Head/Brain
- Tension headaches or migraines
- Feeling wired but tired
- Emotional whiplash — from peaceful to panicked
- Feeling dissociated or floaty

Face/Jaw/Neck
- Lump-in-throat feeling
- Tight jaw from holding back emotion
- Skin crawling or overstimulation

Chest
- Racing heart or pounding chest
- Sudden rushes of heat or cold
- Internal buzzing (nerves lit up)
- Breath holding or chest tightness
- Feeling unsafe in your own body

Abdomen/Gut
- Nausea
- Stomach tension
- Gut tightness or fluttering
- Craving grounding (wanting to lay flat)

Arms/Hands
- Tingling in the hands
- Jittery, shaky, or restless sensations
- Flinching at sudden noises
- Sensory overload (touch sensitivity)

Legs/Feet
- Heavy limbs
- Weighted-down or dragging sensation
- Shakiness post-cry or rage release
- Craving grounding
- Inability to sit still, restlessness

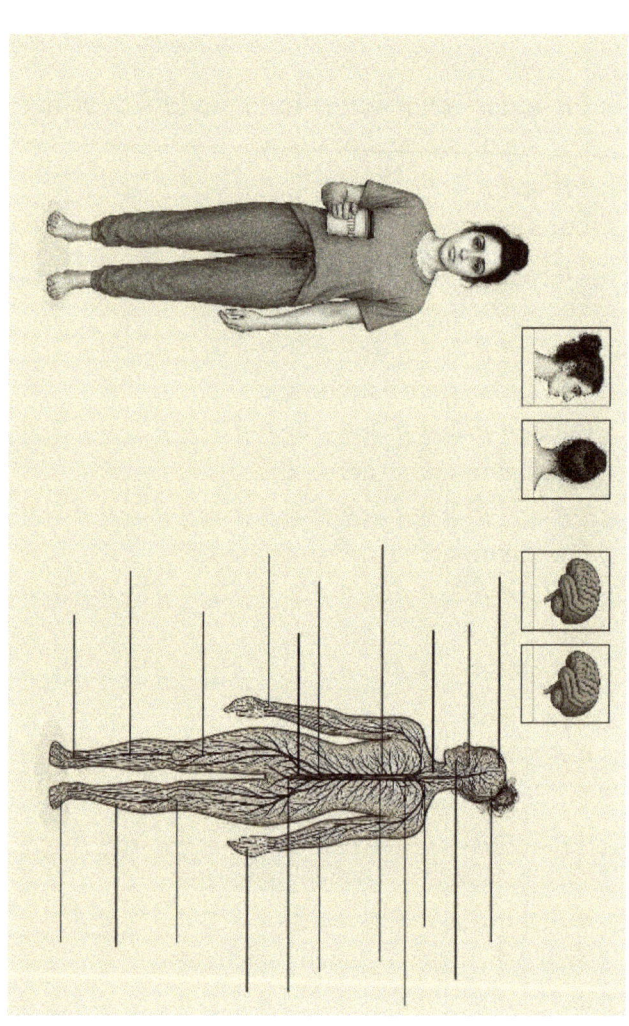

Emotions—Feelings—Sensations

Head/Brain:
- Overwhelmed
- Anxious
- Hyper-alert
- Crying for no reason

Face/Jaw/Neck:
- Skin crawling from overstimulation
- Exhaustion that feels bone-deep
- Impatience
- Touched-out

Chest:
- Love so big it feels like heartbreak
- Guilt
- Fear of doing it wrong
- Heaviness

Abdomen/Gut:
- Gut tension or tingles
- Disconnection from body
- Confused
- Burnout

Arms/Hands:
- Roller rage (outbursts)
- Sensory overload
- Frustration from constant caregiving
- Touched-out

Legs/Feet:
- Groundlessness
- Longing for rest
- Physical exhaustion
- Loneliness in stillness

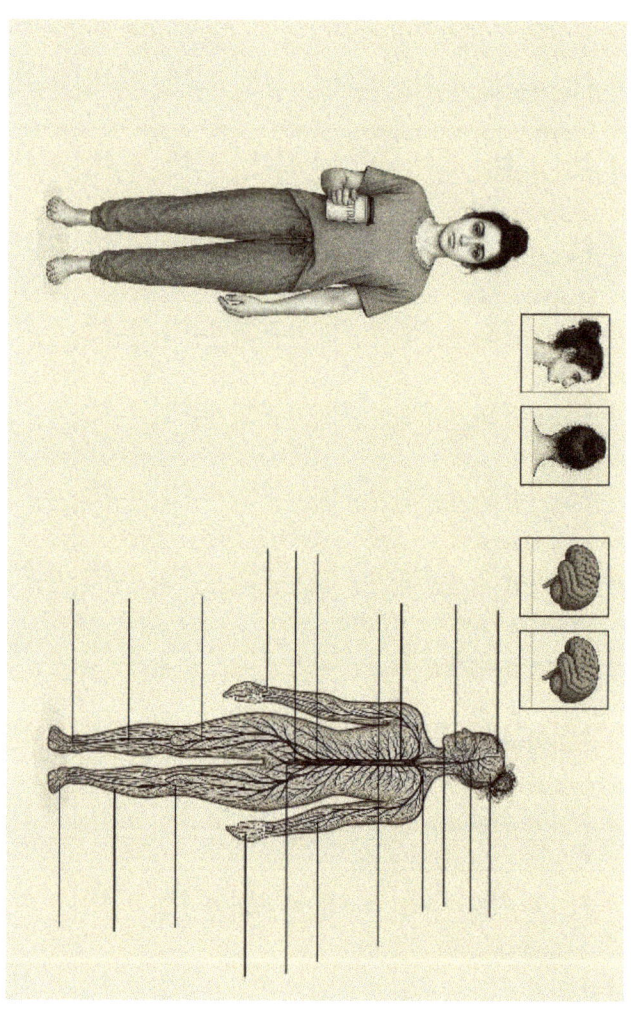

Chapter 5

Built In The Breaking — That's Where She Rose

I didn't find her all at once.

There was no grand awakening.
No mirror moment where I locked eyes with myself and
thought, "I'm back."

It was quieter than that.
Subtle. Gentle.
But undeniable.

It was a flicker.

The first time I laughed — from the belly — and didn't feel
guilt immediately after.
The first time I got dressed in something that felt like me,
caught my reflection, and felt the shift:
"She's still in here."

Not back.
Not returned.
But emerging.

It wasn't every day.
It wasn't even most days.
But when those flickers came?
They meant everything.

Not because they brought me "back."
But because they reminded me:

I was never gone.

I had just gone deeper.

Buried under duty.
Pressed down by pain.
Tucked away beneath everything I had to carry just to keep
going.

But like any seed in the dark,
I wasn't broken.

I was becoming.

And maybe that's the most sacred part of it all —
Realizing that this version of me, this emerging self,
wasn't returning from something...

She was rising through it.

This wasn't about bouncing back.
This was about breaking open.

And yeah — it's hard.
It's unfair.
It bends you in ways no one talks about.

But damn — what comes through that kind of breaking?

It's built to last.

This isn't the girl I used to be.

This is the woman I grew into.

Planted.
Pressed.
Pulled through.
And finally — starting to bloom.

Healing didn't feel like a comeback.
It felt like catching sparks in the dark.

Tiny flares of self —
a hot coffee I didn't reheat three times.
A playlist that made my blood move again.
A short walk where I actually looked at the sky.
A book that pulled me out of my world and into possibility.
Lip gloss on my lips just because it made me feel a little closer
to center.

These moments didn't save me.
They reminded me:
You still matter. You still have a spark.

There's a moment in healing when you realize:

The armour you wore to survive —
the bracing, the guarding, the gritting your teeth —
protected you.

But it also trapped you.

It kept you safe when everything was raw.
But safety isn't the same as peace.

And I was ready for peace.

I started loosening my grip.
Softening the edges.
Letting strength look like rest instead of resistance.

And slowly, I stopped trying to go back.

Because I wasn't meant to return to the girl I was before.

I was meant to become.

Becoming doesn't arrive all at once.
It arrives in pieces.

Through stillness.
Through sweat.
Through breath.
Through breakdowns in the laundry room and breakthroughs
in the car with music blasting louder than my thoughts.

And somewhere in the middle of the mess…
I felt it.

That flicker of HER.
The woman I was always meant to be —
not polished, not perfect — but powerful.

The storms ran out of rain.
The clouds finally cracked.
And I looked around, still standing — not untouched, but
undone and rebuilt.

This time, healing wasn't about holding it all together.

It was about releasing what I never needed to carry.
It was about remembering that rising isn't about being ready.

It's about choosing it anyway.

"The flicker was enough to start a fire."
— A mama rising in her own time

Question for You:
What small moment reminded you that your fire isn't gone
— it's just waiting to be reignited?
How can you fan that spark today, even a little?

Pause & Process Page:

Honour the flickers.
Stack the sparks.
Build your new beginning — one breath, one step, one dream at a time.

I didn't rebuild all at once.

But piece by piece, spark by spark,
I rose through the breaking.

Because the real becoming didn't happen when I avoided the cracks —
it happened when I let the breaking build me.

The storm didn't destroy me.

It built me.

And now?

Now it's time to rise.

Chapter 6

This is Her Becoming

I didn't find her all at once.

There was no grand awakening.
No mirror moment where I locked eyes with myself and
thought, "I'm back."

It was quieter than that.
Subtle. Gentle.
But undeniable.

It was a flicker.

She was emerging.

It wasn't every day.
It wasn't even most days.
But when those flickers came?
They meant everything.

Like a seed in the dark,
I wasn't broken.
I was becoming.

"Becoming isn't about arriving somewhere or achieving a
certain aim. It's a forward motion, a means of evolving, a way
to reach continuously toward a better self."
— Michelle Obama

And maybe that's the most sacred part of all—
realizing that this version of me,
this emerging self,
wasn't returning from something...

She was rising through it.

"The transition to motherhood is not an on-off switch. It's a
process — one that unfolds slowly, with flickers of identity
returning and shifting."

— Dr. Alexandra Sacks

You don't rise from postpartum like a phoenix from ashes.
You rise like a woman who's earned her fire.

Who's walked through it.
Who's held the screaming child and the screaming heart at
the same time—
and kept going.

This moment?
This is HER arrival.

Not the old her.
Not the exhausted shell of her.
But the unfolding of a woman with fire in her bones
and wisdom in her scars.

"I've had to learn to make room for all the parts of me. Not just the strong ones, but the scared, the healing, and the growing parts, too."
— Serena Williams

This is where the shift happens.
When the fog starts to lift
and the voice inside says:

"Look at you. You made it this far.
And you're just getting started."

It's not soft.
It's not delicate.
It's rich.
It's earned.

You are not breaking anymore.
You're building.

And everything you need?
It's already inside you now.

The strength.
The softness.
The grit.
The grace.

You've carried it all.

Now—
you get to rise with it.

"You either walk inside your story and own it, or you stand outside your story and hustle for your worthiness."
— Brené Brown

"There is no greater gift you can give or receive than to honor your calling. It's why you were born. And how you become most truly alive."
— Oprah Winfrey

"I didn't come back stronger. I came back truer."
— A mama who rose from the wreckage

Question for You:
What have you been through that shaped you more than it shattered you?
What did you learn in the breaking that you couldn't have found any other way?

Pause & Process Page:
This is where she rose.
Not after the storm — but inside it.
Honor what you've been through.
Name what you've grown into.
And take a moment to say:
I made it here. And I'm still rising.

Chapter 7

Denim, Lip Gloss & Lattes — The Comeback Era

"She didn't bounce back. She stepped forward like she owned the damn runway."

This is the era of big energy and bold beauty.
Not for anyone else.
Not to prove a thing.

This is about HER.

The woman rebuilt from scratch.
The one who walked through postpartum flames and came out with her own damn glow.

This chapter?
It smells like espresso.
It shines like a fresh swipe of gloss.
And baby—it wears denim like armour dipped in softness.

You know that feeling?

When you slip on the jeans—the ones that hug you in all the right places,
that move with your body, not against it,
that say "She's back" without needing to shout?

That's this chapter.

This is the comeback.
And no, not a return to who you were—
but the reveal of who you've been becoming all along.

Denim.
Lip gloss.
Lattes.
Call them accessories.
Call them rituals.
I call them tools.

Tools that helped me reconnect with my body, my mood, my edge, my light.

• Denim: My power skin. Resilient. Worn in. Ready for anything.
• Lip gloss: One swipe = instant energy. Sparkle. Sass. Sex appeal. Softness.
• Latte: Warmth. Ritual. A slow sip of "I'm worth it."
• Self-tan? The only thing I'm faking—and even that's a wink-wink flex.

This isn't shallow.
This is fashion psychology.

What you wear changes how you feel.
The textures on your skin, the colours on your body, the way your clothes move—
they speak to your nervous system.

They remind you:
You're not just surviving.
You're creating. You're expressing. You're RISING.

It's not about the clothes.
It's about the feeling they unlock.

This comeback era?

It's not loud.
It's confident.

It walks into the room like she knows exactly who she is.
Because she does.

It's lipstick on a Monday.
It's jeans that make you feel like you could take over the world.
It's a latte carried like a trophy.
It's laughing louder.
It's taking up space.
It's knowing damn well that you are the moment.

"I don't shine because I'm never broken. I shine because I rise glittering from the pieces."
— Tracee Ellis Ross

Question for You:
• What's your power piece right now? That thing that helps you feel like YOU again?

• If your comeback had a look, a scent, a mood, a soundtrack—what would it be?

Pause & Process Page:
This is your comeback era.
Say it. Write it. Wear it.
Shine like hell and sip that latte like the soft badass you are.

The comeback wasn't the end.

It was the beginning of a new kind of strength—
One that didn't need to scream.
One that didn't demand attention.
One that radiated from the inside out.

Soft.
Steady.
Unshakeable.

Chapter 8

Fashion Psychology — The Revolution Of Becoming

This isn't about trends.
It's not about what's "in" this season.
This is a personal revolution.

This is fashion as identity, energy, and nervous system support.
This is becoming HER through the clothes you choose and how they make you feel.

Postpartum shifted everything.
And while the world kept telling me to "bounce back,"
I decided to lean forward.

I wasn't looking to reclaim who I was.
I was dressing to step into who I was becoming.

Every texture, colour, and layer became a signal to my nervous system:
You're safe. You're strong. You're HER.

I didn't need to look put together.
I needed to feel grounded, aligned, and soft—like I was beginning to recognize the woman I was growing into.

What touches your skin changes how you carry yourself.

The Frequency of Fabric

Researcher Heidi Yellen studied fabric frequencies—literally, how materials vibrate.

- Linen and wool: Over 5,000 Hz
- Cotton and silk: Still high frequency
- Synthetics: 0 Hz — they give you nothing

Your skin feels that.
Your nervous system absorbs that.
So if that polyester top feels like static?
It's not just uncomfortable—it's disruptive.

Style Is Psychology

Fashion psychologist Shakaila Forbes-Bell confirms what many of us instinctively know:

- Clothes influence confidence, mood, cognition, and emotional regulation
- What we wear can stimulate dopamine
- "Enclothed cognition" is real — dressing with intention shifts your mental state

Soft Armour, Real Advice

Fashion isn't about being fancy.
It's about feeling better.

And in postpartum? That's everything.

Start here:
- Matching sets — give your brain visual order & your body a sense of effortlessness
- One-pieces/jumpsuits — no decisions required, just slide in and go
- Soft leggings + loose tops — still practical, but feel-good layering matters
- Fabrics you want to touch — think brushed cotton, bamboo, ribbed knits
- Color matters — reach for shades that energize, calm, or uplift you

And when you shop?

- Ask: How does this feel on my skin?
- Ask: Can I breathe in this?
- Ask: Does this support the HER I'm becoming?

This isn't about dressing up.
It's about dressing inward.

Your closet can be a healing tool.
Your clothes can be a love language to yourself.

Fashion becomes your soft armor when it holds you through motherhood,
anchors your spirit on chaotic days,

and lets you feel beautiful on the inside and the outside.

"My fashion has always been driven by my mood, and my mood was on mom mode for a minute."
— Rihanna

"When you wear something you love, it shows up in how you move, how you speak, and how you treat yourself."
— Shakaila Forbes-Bell

Question for You:

- What textures, fabrics, or pieces feel like "soft armor" to you?
- What outfit makes you feel like HER—even on a hard day?
- How does your wardrobe reflect your healing?

Pause & Process Page:
Write your style story.
List your favourite go-to pieces for comfort, strength, and identity.
Imagine what SHE wears on her best day—then start dressing in that direction.

Chapter 9

Crown On, Cape Out

You're not lost.

You're not broken.

You're not trying to "get back to her."

You are becoming. And SHE is a fking force.

There is no rewind in postpartum. No return trip to who you were.

Because that woman—beautiful as she was—

Had no idea how strong you were about to become.

This isn't about surviving anymore.

It's about showing up.

Not for the world.

Not for a performance.

For you.

This is your homecoming.

Crown on. Cape out.

Let's Be Clear

You've been through it.

You bled. You stretched. You broke down. You stitched yourself back together while feeding a baby and answering texts and trying to remember if you even brushed your teeth. You did all of that on no sleep and with a body that didn't feel like your own.

You smiled when it hurt.

You kept going when you didn't know how.

You held your baby, your family, your home, your damn self together—

And the world just kept spinning like it was nothing.

But it was everything.

The things you've done, the storms you've walked through, the resilience it took to stand up again every single day—

That's strength. That's grit. That's what SHE is made of.

The Power of the Unseen

There are no medals for the middle of the night.

No bonus checks for diaper runs and doctor calls.

No standing ovation when you finally get your toddler to eat one damn vegetable.

But hear this:

"You have done a million invisible things that made the world go round—and no one clapped. So clap for your damn self."

You became everything and then some.

You learned how to run on fumes and still give your baby safety, comfort, warmth.

You learned how to think three steps ahead even while breaking inside.

You became a walking lifeline.

No training. No breaks. No map.

And still—you did it. You are doing it.

Now Look Up

You're standing in the mirror and something's different.

The lines on your face, the weight on your hips, the storm behind your eyes… it all tells a story.

But so does this:

You're not just standing—you're rooted.

Clearer. Wiser. Unshakeably HER.

You see flickers of your fire coming back.

The comeback smile. The unbothered shrug. The quiet knowing.

You've stopped trying to be who you were.

Because you've outgrown her.

You built a new woman—and she fits like hell.

This Is HER Now

She doesn't play small.

She doesn't beg to be seen.

She's not worried about bouncing back or fitting in.

She's not hiding.

She's arriving.

You wear the cape now—not to rescue—but to remind them:

You already won.

"You're not tired because you're weak. You're tired because you've been strong as hell for too long without being celebrated."

So here's the celebration.

This chapter. These words. This moment.

This is the standing ovation.

Final Word to You

You don't need fixing.

You don't need a "glow-up."

You don't need permission.

You already did the hardest thing a human can do.

You brought life into the world—and somehow managed to keep yours going, too.

You are the proof.

That strength can look like softness.

That motherhood is a full-body transformation—of mind,
spirit, identity, and soul.
You are the revolution.
The shift.
The reason this book is going to move the damn earth.
Crown on.
Cape out.
SHE has arrived.

Chapter 10

HER

"She remembered who SHE was — and the game changed."

There comes a moment —
after the chaos,
after the quiet,
after the crawl-back-from-the-edge days —

Where you don't just remember who you are.
You reclaim HER.
You become HER.

Not the girl from before.
Not the version you curated to be liked, accepted, or
understood.
Not the woman they expected you to shrink into.

But the one who lived through the fire.
Walked through hell.
And came back dressed in strength and sacred confidence.
Unraveled. Unchained. Fully embodied.

This is HER anointing.
HER homecoming.

This is where SHE lets go of the reins and lets HERSELF feel
it all.
Where SHE no longer hides from HER own power.

Where SHE finally says — "I made it. And now I rise."

This chapter is for HER.

For the woman still waking up from survival mode.
For the mother who cried on the bathroom floor and still stood up to make breakfast.
For the one who looked in the mirror and thought — "Is this it?"
Only to find out later:
No. This is the rise.

"There were moments I wanted to give up. But I didn't.
Because something in me — HER — refused to die there."
— A woman reborn

This is for the woman who didn't fake it —
SHE FAITHED IT.
SHE fought forward through fog, fear, and identity loss.

SHE didn't need to earn HER way back to HERSELF.
Because SHE wasn't out there waiting.
SHE was inside — buried under the survival and the silence
— but never gone.

"Becoming a mom was the biggest transition of my life. I had to rebuild my identity — piece by piece."
— Serena Williams

SHE is the woman who:

- Rebuilt HERSELF with shaking hands and a defiant heart.
- Showed up even when no one clapped.
- Held HER babies while HER body still felt broken.
- Let go of everything that asked HER to shrink.
- Chose softness as power, not weakness.
- Danced with HER shadows and still chose joy.
- Stopped apologizing for taking up space.
- Named HERSELF enough — and meant it.

Becoming HER wasn't a fairytale sunrise.
It was bloody. bold. relentless.

It happened in the quiet moments when SHE whispered:
"Not today. Not my story."
In the scream behind the steering wheel.
In the prayer choked out mid-shower.
In the decision to keep going — not because SHE had to,
but because SHE was done abandoning herself.

And even on the days that aren't great —
There is still good.
There are still blessings.
Look for them. Count them.

Hold your babies.
Look into their eyes and feel the pieces of you that they
helped uncover —
The parts you buried to survive,
The stories your soul tucked away,

The healing that comes only when you're cracked wide open by love.

They're not just yours — they are pieces of your soul walking outside your body.
They remind you what matters.
They call you forward.
They show you the HER you're becoming.

If you have a spouse who sees you — really sees you —
Who stands by you and chooses Team You through it all,
Hold them close.
Thank the stars.
There's grace in being loved like that.
There's power in receiving it.

"I didn't know who I was. I literally lost myself. I would look in the mirror and not even recognize my own reflection."
— Chrissy Teigen

Motherhood isn't for the faint of heart.

It's brutal and beautiful.
It's messy and miraculous.
It's wild, silly, sacred, and full of love that explodes from places you didn't even know existed.

And through it all —
SHE rises.

YOU ARE HER.

Not because you're polished.
Not because you always smile now.
Not because life finally makes sense.

You are HER because you refused to stay buried.
Because you chose to rise.
Because you kept building a future — even when you
couldn't fully see it.

"I had really bad postpartum depression after I had my son,
and it frightened me. I felt very inadequate; I felt like I'd
made the worst decision of my life."
— Adele

SHE isn't about perfection.
SHE is born in the breakdowns.
Built in the bounce-backs.
Reclaimed in the moments no one sees.

This isn't the end.
This is the beginning of HER era.

The era where:
• SHE walks into rooms without shrinking.
• SHE claims softness as strength.
• SHE laughs harder, cries deeper, and lives louder.
• SHE builds a life that doesn't just look good — but feels
good.

"When HER soul whispered 'go, 'SHE listened — and built the life that once felt out of reach."

One to live by:
SHE didn't just find HERSELF — SHE built HERSELF.
— A woman who rose, loved, led, and soared

Question for You:
• Who is SHE to you?
• How will you honour HER — today, tomorrow, and every damn day after?

Pause & Process Page
Write a letter to HER.
Thank HER.
Tell HER you see her now.
Tell HER you're never leaving her again.

Final Words from Me to You:
You didn't lose yourself.
You didn't ruin anything.
You weren't too much.

You were becoming.

You rose into the fiercest, most radiant version of YOU —
Even if the weight is still there.
Even if healing takes time.
Even if joy and grief still share the same breath.

You are already HER.

The world is better because you pushed on.
Because you believed.
Because you kept rising — even when it hurt.

I am so proud of you.
Keep going.
Keep building.
Keep becoming.

You were built for this.
You are HER.
Always.

www.ingramcontent.com/pod-product-compliance
Lightning Source LLC
Chambersburg PA
CBHW051233120626
46547CB00013B/1617